Until We Are Level Again

FIRST EDITION, 2018

Until We Are Level Again
© 2018 by José Angel Araguz

ISBN 978-0-9972517-9-1

Except for fair use in reviews and/or scholarly considerations, no part of this book may be reproduced, performed, recorded, or otherwise transmitted without the written consent of the author
and
the permission of the publisher.

Cover Art & Design
© 2018 by Ani Schreiber

Author Photo
@2018 by Ani Schreiber

Mongrel Empire Press
Norman, OK

Online catalogue: www.mongrelempire.org

This publisher is a proud member of

COUNCIL OF LITERARY MAGAZINES & PRESSES
w w w . c l m p . o r g

Contents

One
Gloves	1
Between Us A Hummingbird	2
Letter (white)	3
The Story of the Prisoner Who Made Friends with a Sparrow	4
Letter (crucifixes)	5
Tantalus in Matamoros	6
Learning Objects	7
Late	8
Jodido	9

Two
Dandelions	13
The Ladder	14
Letter (clouds)	15
Escape Ropes	16
Street Performer	17
Marked	18
Letter (work)	19
Small Talk	20
Hell's Kitchen	21
The Broken Escalator at the Train Platform	22

Three
Letter (key dream)	25
Another Sound	26
Blue Ode	27
The Wall	28

Four
Burial Clothes	45
Theology at Work	46
Element	47
Correspondence	48
Last Rites	49
Old Man in a Rocker	50
La Esquina	51
Corpus Christi	52
On Monet's The Red Kerchief, Portrait of Mrs. Monet	53
Gentleman	54

Hansel	55
Letter (the wall revisited)	56
Bird Hunger	57
Speaking Spanish on the Streets of NYC	58
Acknowledgements	60

Until We Are Level Again

José Angel Araguz

2018

ONE

Gloves

I made up a story for myself once,
that each glove I lost
was sent to my father in prison;

that's all it would take for him
to chart my growth without pictures
without words or visits,

only colors and design,
texture; it was ok then
for skin to chafe and ash,

to imagine him
trying on a glove,
stretching it out

my open palm closing
and disappearing
in his fist.

Between Us A Hummingbird

The indecipherable tiny heart
of each moment between a man
and a woman, later father and mother,

later words on paper–miles
from the river the mother crossed,
each breath taking flight–returning

to the air the father died in,
prison bars lining his last sky
blue lines on paper the son beats

his hand across in ink and pressure —
from tongue to tongue, accent to stress,
the air keeps breaking, the river runs,

indecipherable, each blurred moment
on the wings of another —

LETTER (WHITE)
after Li Po

The moon fills the river with the white of hair yet to be doled out. I stand, and it passes. I turn, and it comes. I kneel to see my face, and instead see many faces. White ripples to white waves, to white that keeps turning away.

>Father who never grew into your white, tell me:
>How many fathers in this water?

THE STORY OF THE PRISONER WHO MADE FRIENDS WITH A SPARROW

My father digging
for grubs and snails, eating
his bread only enough
to leave crumbs on his palm,
his hand out each morning
through the bars, holding out
whatever he has found
for the flutter that knows him,
the eyes that never meet his,
that look around him,
for him, a child's eyes
almost, unable to place
or name a father,
only take
what he can spare,
and move on.

LETTER (CRUCIFIXES)

When Jesus's hands return, and his face appears again without expression, it is you I see, come back into this world as I last saw you: shirtless, all ribs and outstretched arms, halted behind the prison courtyard's chain-link fence.

> Father I reach for and am held back from:
> am I serving
> the sentence started
> with the end of your life?

Tantalus in Matamoros

Before he died, my mother took me
to see my father in prison.
After saying hello,
I was hushed and kept aside.

What words he spoke and cried over,
what forgivenesses
he asked—I reach for them
and pull back different words each time.

With this memory, I grow
thin, less and less of me
stoops, trying to drink of
these waters. When they recede,

the story of a man left to longing
returns, to be told in human breath.

LEARNING OBJECTS

Before truth, my mother's stagger
back into our shared room
after waitressing late.

Before time, the wordless drop
of her body
into bed beside me.

Before rhetoric, a song on her lips
as she settled in beside me,
and her far away voice.

Later, the counterpoint of car keys in her hand,
each meaningful shift and crook.

Later, the interjection of a slammed door,
and the pathetic fallacy of the sunrise.

In each reusable entity called a word,
there are things we think we can hold;
later, only things we try to hold.

LATE

In the dresses she wore for work,
my mother became the front yard
we went without. Their dense fabric
stitched with bright designs,

flowers and leaves arranged to greet
the customers of Rosita's on Morgan,
not there anymore, but I know,
as dense as I've become, nothing

matters beyond first impressions:
the apron hanging off the door;
the iron hissing in her hand,
late, but insistent to look good;

my mother's face bright, steadfast
as light through a threadbare sheet
held over the face of a child
pretending to be asleep.

JODIDO

For my mother, this word lies
between cracked sun-hardened skin
and being all out of luck.

This word a summary
of months tallied in gray hairs
where she wanted to be angry
but dusted old photos instead.

This word her word
for me at twenty-two
going hungry and disappearing—
She might as well be shouting my name,
calling me out of my sleeping bag in the living room
to see her off,
my six-year-old arms reaching high around
her black apron,
the color worn
to the smoke it reeks of,
her pen and pad snug in the pockets
curled against me,
Sweet 'N Low packets snapping
like the broken claps of leaves
when she would walk to the car
and thunder off
in the unanimous roar
of gravel.

Two

Dandelions

As a child, I looked at them
as though they were made
of the most beautiful dust.

When I later heard of a man
returning to dust, I imagined
a head shaking

with a sudden laughter,
undone on the wind,
dust lifting to the sky,

specks
outnumbering the stars.

THE LADDER
for Christine Maloy

In a difficult time
the ladder grows different,
thinner. A wind comes
and sways what you hold onto.

A bee in the grass — I've stumbled
like that on the page. Drunk,
one would say. Staggering.
Unfocused. Searching.

When a friend dies you haven't
spoken to in years,
the ladder has a rung
a different color, you struggle
to think where you first saw it.

Easy to say dust.
Easy to say we are dust.
A bit harder to say
where the ladder leads to.

The proper tribute — who
could write it? The lesson of
the ladder grows different,
one would say: staggering.
A different color, you struggle
where the ladder leads to.

LETTER (CLOUDS)

At the foot of the moon, purple clouds. On nights like this, my aunt would find my eyes in the rearview mirror, say: "Esas nubes son ovejas que han perdido el camino." We'd be driving home from her shift at P.O.E.T.S. on Saratoga, and I'd be cold from having lain awake trying to see past streetlamp and cloud to the stars from the backseat.

Tonight, purple clouds exactly when she said these words about sheep losing their way. Purple clouds my waiting, as if holding my breath again, and letting my eyes water. Purple clouds and holds over me as I come back to these words alone, under the same moon.

> Father of nights never shared:
> How lost can we be
> if we look so much alike?

ESCAPE ROPES

Hands raw from setting knots
the few inches apart it takes
for a leg to imagine a ladder,
ropes designed for escape from a fire
on an oil rig squatted on the gulf,
my mind would work out
images of men with only the open water
to swim, to march across if they could,
to bob and pray for miracles.

Those knotted afternoons,
the sun made an oven of the warehouse.
The foreman stood me in the back
while other men sat on stools
and looked over, faces worn,
fingernails yellowed from smoking.
There, I held my tongue,
grunted against each wince,
and felt fire in my hands.

STREET PERFORMER

Blink and you become a child,
beholden to your eyes to tell the truth.

If seeing is believing, then God has been painted gold
and caught mid-step, yawning in New Orleans.

Blink again, and a nostril flares,
a stray hair needles into the sky.

A dollar bill falls into the cup at His feet; a camera flashes,
the sound like chewing gum smacked between teeth.

Bright arms land at His side like birds;
somebody yells: Get a real job!

We are all witness to something of the second coming
in those slumped shoulders smoldering with light.

When we shake hands, He calls me brother and leaves gold
glinting off my skin like flames seething to ash.

MARKED

My aunt, whose hands
spent mornings and afternoons

patting down dough
and rolling out tortillas,

one after another for hours,
would stand over me

and play the game
of squeezing my hand

in a fist
and laughing,

both of us wondering
how much I could take,

how much I would flail
and burn

in that grip,
all of a day's work

wrenched around
my child hand

just another thing
to muscle

and roll out
into the world,

another thing
to be marked by fire.

LETTER (WORK)

I don't believe in heaven, I believe in work. Work is what kept mom able to live past leaving you, live past seeing you reflected in my changing face. Work is what kept my aunt from feeling helpless. Work kept me quiet and alone in garage apartments as I waited for them to come home long into night. Work breaks us down, exhausts us into our undeniable selves.

When a coworker at a coffee shop in NYC calls our workspace "the lion's den," my mind gets going. Coffee rushing into a paper cup more and more sounds like a whip. The near imperceptible groan as a plastic lid fits onto a cup feels like a part of me. Coins fall into the tip jar like stones into a river made of stones.

> Father who remains undefined yet undeniable:
> What keeps me going with this work
> of pacing across language
> as if it were a home?

Small Talk

At work, we find ourselves
with silences, and, because we're
strangers, we turn to the weather,
or a movie only one of us
has seen, pass the time
in this half way. Today,
we talk bagels, how they
should be cut with the tool
made for the task, yet,
it is obvious to others that
the only real way to do it
is to take a knife
and sideways run it through,
this way the halves are loose
and free, like a wheel
split in two. And this is
why one doesn't talk poetry
with poets: because no matter
how well one has it in hand
someone's bound to find
another way it should've
been done, and so on, back
and forth, until these silences
repair themselves, and we slowly
realize how small the words
are between us.

Hell's Kitchen

There will always be men in the windows of restaurants
stacking chairs like hands on top of each other
and leaving tables clean and clear as sleeping faces.

Men with rags for hands.
Men with hair of fallen elm leaves
who stop to watch faces
roll by in the windows of taxicabs.
Men who swear by the rain
and the slick chisping of tires and street,
by the trail of sparks behind each taillight.

    And you will never have to be here, whoever you are,
never have to taste the mix of gutter and exhaust,
never have to walk into the street, stand in the middle,
and see the nothing coming from one direction
and the nothing coming from the other direction,
never have to walk propelled by the nothing in front of you
leaving you no farther from the nothing you leave behind,

never have to follow the light of streetlamps,
their broken mouths swollen with moths.

The Broken Escalator at the Train Platform

When something like this breaks, it means
we must swarm around the narrow
stairway, our steps slower, the pace
set according to our sighs. Each
glance and gesture becomes a word.
My looking down and waiting speaks
to the old woman next to me:
after you. All the stars left in
the sky, all the calls and blinking
messages, the wintered sorrow
of all passing thoughts must now wait
until we are level again —
wait as we take turns returning
to our lives. When something like this
breaks, it means the words I wanted
to write before are different from
the ones I have got down for you.
These words are older than you think.

Three

LETTER (KEY DREAM)

In which I guide the metal, shave it down, follow the make of another key snapped where one would hold it, and when done, turn to face a door I remember from a neighborhood I never lived in but visited once to hear stories of my father, a door that is locked when I try the handle so that I pull out the new key, and when that jams, begin talking to myself, and stop only to lift a key ring from my side, slide the new key next to a hundred others, and let my arm fall, the key ring hitting my side in a dark chuckle.

Another Sound

For words, there is no equivalent
of the archaeologist's pots
and bits of shield. No crude ax
of a curse; no rumor lingers
in lines of stretched leather; beyond
the earliest evidence of writing, no murmur.

With nothing to parse, what groans
uttered when the first night fell,
and what laughter at the first hands cupped
to hold and spill their reflection in water
are lost. Father, I've lost your face
and go on grieving in the way I have learned.

From these words,
I imagine another sound,
similar perhaps, and no less human,
     yet no less my own
rising and catching the meaning
of the burb and wim of this water.

BLUE ODE

Toward the end of each winter
the river turns broken blue,
a blue with all blues inside:
the blue of eyes, a star-like blue,
      the blue of veins and bruises.

The color of holding still, that blue,
a gradual hardening that gives
a little more each day I walk
speaking to my dead father and see
      the questions he can't ask—

      Who walks now with my face?
      And who is burdened with my name?
      Who speaks with my voice,
      coming through in blue
           shadows and blue cracks?

Questions grow, and in blue writing
blue lines tense as though the words
would rewrite themselves to answer
in blues broken with each season
      coursing inside me.

The Wall
for José Ángel García

I.

your dying
left me
at a wall

when I walk
I imagine you
on the other side
walking

when I stop
to listen in
you stop too

we are alike, see

sometimes
the wall changes
and is the table
where I sit

when I am full
of listening I tear
another page
from the wall
and put

not my ear
but this hand to it

II.

sometimes the wall is the floor I slept on as a child

I used to stay awake
making out the shapes
of the world I knew

from the lessons
of the sofa and table
I began to believe
the true position in life
was standing still

from the rasped sermons
of the roaches
life was scurry
and halt

there was much to learn
lying there
in the same pose
as you

III.

sometimes the wall is a fence

a wall you can see through

you stood behind

this kind of wall

the last time I saw you,

waving, the wind

between us flaring

the colors

of your face

IV.

as a child I would sit
by the window and read
until someone came home

the sound of a turned page
makes me look up
even now as I sit

still with words
and the silence
I have shared
with windows
all my life

a silence closest
to that between
you and me

I sit on this side
of the wall
able to see
only what is left
in the world

V.

sometimes the wall is the size of my palm

a photograph of your face
a faded color
in that other life

the paper

a flower

curled and breaking

the wall

falling leaving

only my hand

VI.

the mirror: the wall whose paint I am
where I watch myself grow old

forgetting the child
forgetting the father

I almost looked like all my life

VII.

the body, too, is a wall

when I try to hear you
through this wall
all I hear

is the beat
of a shoulder

turning over
bearing down

a man
who cannot rest
until I do

VIII.

when I saw her last
your mother smiled
and called out to me
from where she lay
called out my name
which is your name too
and shook and smiled
not able to see my face
I want to believe
she called out
to both of us
this name
this shared air
between the three of us
turning over
in her stories
in my questions
when I held her hand
her other gripped my arm
touching the body
she could not see
that she had seen
in several shapes
she could flip through
in her memory
photographs of two men
with one name
together there
behind the wall
of her clouded eyes

IX.

silence

the wall we stand against

walk along sleep under

the response of a father

who hears the same thing

when I speak

as when I do not

X.

there were hours I would lay out on the grass
the itch and friction of the earth at my back

I was nearing the age you were when you died
I did my best not to think then
between the sky and land

the wall then was unreachable
I could not see the end of blue
into the stars I knew were there

these days the wall sends the cold
of dirt and roots and stones into me
and reminds me of how
you remain inside the wall
I have my back against

XI.

lined paper
my hand
at white
blinds

at the window again
my hand follows
seems to be forever
hesitant to touch

the pen darkens and guides
my sight my fingers
bent over
each word

each shape

each finger

each twig

each powerline

each crucifix

each jag of barbed wire

points to another wall

XII.

a bird lands near the bench I am sitting on
and fidgets closer to my feet

in the silence between us
is a wall made up of
not knowing one another

this small body
that for a moment
skitters in my direction
does not have
the eyes to place who I am
nor knows words to call to me
yet it lingers
cocks its head
in the grace
given by infants
to their parents
nameless placeless
except for a presence
that cannot be ignored

XIII.

sometimes the wall is a color you cannot see beyond

the white of the breaking ocean in photographs of you

the white of paper where I keep finding you almost

the white between words

the white breath of winter

the white hairs slowly taking over my body

white words that cannot be read yet

> when I turn
> the color of paper
> what will be written on me
>
> my living
> writing

white of the full moon out to harangue the darkness

XIV.

family

stones set in place to hold

until one breaks off

and there is still a wall

but in the place

of the missing

is the shape of the wind

and the tension

of doing without

XV.

sometimes the wall is the face I clear away in the early morning

no soap only water and the glow of a kerosene lamp

I guide the blade for the first time over the curves

so much like yours I have been told

this hair kept by me out of pride to look like you

to mirror the photographs

with this part of me

darkness answering darkness

saluting almost

I feel each tug of the blade cut

until less and less of you remains

across the skin

where light has not fallen for years

where the sun waits to rise

to this other face

raw and jagged

with change

Four

Burial Clothes

The man in the wheelchair flaps his baseball cap,
tells me he likes what I am wearing,

that he has been looking for something
to go with his black leather vest,

that for days he has been thinking about
burial clothes. He turns to cough

and his shirt shifts over his rocker-chair shoulders,
clings to him as it would on a hanger in his closet,

but before he can completely disappear
he goes back to talking, and I let him,

and watch as his words
catch and stretch

over our reflections
on the windows of the bus,

everything passing
covered in breath.

THEOLOGY AT WORK

If there is a heaven
I will buy my way in
with slices of tomato,

with acts like this one,
separating this body from itself,
bringing down the knife

without thinking,
my hands working
in a silence

broken only by the knock
of the blade
when it can go no further

and trails the sluice
of these hours
across a door

that might one day open.

ELEMENT

The wind would be water and fire,
would be earth—sand and gravel,
mud churning, even magma—

as I held my hand out from
the car on drives back to Texas.
The whole time my child hand

bucked and braced—a human flag
that, like everything human, refused
to be itself—I thought the wind

familiar, and made more so by
exposure; enough time,
my hand would turn element.

If in the wind I felt everything
I knew the world to be made of,
then perhaps in the air between

Matamoros and Corpus Christi
the lines of my father's face deepen
as the horizon deepens now

the more the sun sinks into it;
as the lines on this page deepen
as my hand braces into each word.

Correspondence

sin palabras,
el mar viene y se va –
it comes and it goes

LAST RITES

Were I ten years old again
I would have no problem
drawing from memory the words
that made my mother's house
feel bigger in the dark:

the bedroom window wider;
the night quieter in its audience;
my tongue passing over
Spanish it has since mistrusted.
Then I would have cared more

to say what was expected,
would not have paused at
    Padre nuestro,
       que estás en el cielo–
my hand would not have trembled
as it followed through

with the sign of the cross,
a motion I now repeat shakily
over a dead bird on the sidewalk.
I hurry and hope no one sees me,
already in another silence

describing the bird's still head as:
the thumb on the hand of the dead,
drawing from memory the words,
my tongue passing over
    Padre nuestro,
a motion I now repeat shakily.

OLD MAN IN A ROCKER

The fantasies of others are of little interest.
This painting where an old man in a rocker
stares into the sun from his porch

does little for my own unrest,
nor does it change the words I hear
in fantasy. Others are of little interest.

I write: *In the evening's last light, I'm lost* —
it too is less a person, more a color.
Staring into the sun from this porch,

the evening is what the painter's left for us
to guess at. In my eyes, over and over,
are fantasies of other evenings. My interest

in what may have happened stirs summers
inside me: the smell of grass, and no father
staring at the son I am. Soft peach

upon the face; not face but canvas.
Son, God has grown tired of us, I hear
again. *We're fantasies, of little interest
except as stairs rising into the sun.*

La Esquina

In the mirror over the bar,
I see myself for a moment,
then blur to another shape,

another man holding a bottle
the color of his skin,
laughing, sure,

only it looks like wincing
as part of himself
leaves his lips,

returns silent, eyes rimmed
with light: the eyes of a dog
waiting out a fire.

Corpus Christi

Summer's last hope on the edge of the window screen:
    the roach who flits his wings and tries,

higher, then lower, to get through. The rest content
    to scour books and hide in the copper

of my jar of pennies. Or dangle off coat hangers
    in the closet. Or sleep a dark sleep

in the corners of the ceiling. Wherever stuck — no twitch
    of antennae to translate the match struck

for the oil lamp's wick, or my belt buckle's chime,
    or even the sound of pages turned

as a reason to move — they become shadow. This late,
    I hardly dare to move either.

The scratching at the screen dies. This one is learning,
    has smacked himself to frustration.

Will he, like the rest, lie down in what there is,
    and become shadow? Will I be here,

my brown wings tucked away, with only these focused
    forms of attention to confide in?

On Monet's The Red Kerchief, Portrait of Mrs. Monet

That red was everything,
that face, the turn of the head

as if she heard him
not calling her back.

The world at the window,
snow swirling, collapsing, cold—

could he feel
her small want

burning through
the pane of glass,

or is this not the story:
was he, like me,

merely at work,
prodding at something

he could only recall
in pieces, each stroke

a guess, a question
gathering itself

in the two black pebbles
sinking in a puddle of gray

that to me
are her eyes.

GENTLEMAN

As his eyes follow each beat across each heart monitor,

    each flinch on the face of a man

        going eighty on the freeway

    when his cigarette drops,

Death—gentleman who dog-eared the eyes of my father

    as he died in prison

        and stuffed what he would have said to me

    down into dark pockets –

slips blank pages throughout the stories I write,

    and leaves black spots where I would remember,

        where I falter after

    what the rude word might be

        that leaves the night done,

makes the birds fall.

HANSEL

to his muse

I do not know why
I give the earth these phrases,
sounds, thoughts,
all broken off in pieces
that trail behind.

Do I expect to find my way,
to look back and have it all
come together, or will I see
that I have led myself into darkness?

Listen — each footstep
cackles with the words
of twigs and dry leaves.

Hold me, sister,
and tell me when we are almost there,
when everything behind us disappears,
when home is what we walk toward

and these words are the sun
cracking through branches,
the forest dissolving
in light.

LETTER (THE WALL REVISITED)

In ancient Egypt, there was a practice of painting cloth sheets to wrap around coffins, and a belief that the soul would not rest until this task was done, until this last wall, behind which the dead were wound up by the living, was in place.

I write:

> *steadfast*
> *as light through a threadbare sheet*
> *held over the face of a child*
> *pretending to be asleep—*

and a friend remarks that he sees a dead body implied. This, within an image of me as a child.

I write you this and you cannot hear it. I write you this and you cannot ask questions. I write you this and all I can hear are questions I cannot ask.

> Father, kin to me in silence,
> at this sheet I work the colors of my living
> and ask: *Whose soul?*

BIRD HUNGER

And what makes up ever after?
Birds flying free from the rubble.

One, the bird before the pie goes in the oven
clawing at the crust, unable to get out.

Another, the bird possessed by intuition
knowing exactly which wicked sister's eye to gouge.

My mother and father became strangers;
their silence became the waters of my memories.

I am the bird flying out of the waters
singing of everything that has happened.

My flight is hunger; my song is questions. I have no choice
but to keep on in a tale in which I can never go home.

SPEAKING SPANISH ON THE STREETS OF NYC

I want to believe they are not speaking Spanish,
this mother and son so much like the mother and son
in photographs back in Texas, but they are. I want to believe
the boy has lost no father, the mother never had to explain
being broke nor how bodies break, that they speak
only sunlight, speak held hands, speak city traffic,
speak flags of many countries. I want to believe they are not
filled with the same words in which I lost my father,
words my mother cried through later, explaining
about a man she left and how she'd never leave me,
the same words shuffled out as I explained I had to leave –
      words moving the air between us, words holding
            over the miles, words letting through all we mean
      to each other — I want to believe, but know they speak
in the same words I have to keep to myself,
words mumbled in the park, taking the shape of
Mi vida es una rama que, a tu paso, deshojas;
I know the words they speak, but not what the words mean
between the stranger I am now and this mother and son.

                                after Pedro Miguel Obligado

Acknowledgements

Special thanks to the editors of the following publications where the poems noted were published, sometimes in earlier versions:

The 2River View: "Between Us A Hummingbird" "Street Performer" & "Hansel."

The Acentos Review: "Hell's Kitchen"

Apple Valley Review: "Late" "Small Talk" "Blue Ode" & "Gentleman"

Blue Collar Review: "Escape Ropes"

The Boiler Journal: "The Broken Escalator at the Train Platform"

Borderlands: Texas Poetry Review: "Letter (white)" & "Tantalus in Matamoros"

Cider Press Review: "Corpus Christi"

El Mono (monopoem series): "Letter (clouds)"

Glass: "Theology at Work" & "Speaking Spanish on the Streets of NYC"

Gris-Gris: "The Ladder" & "Letter (work)"

The Merrimack Review: "La Esquina"

The Oklahoma Review: "Dandelions"

The Olduvain Review: "Another Sound"

Poet Lore: "Jodido" & "Marked"

Rattle: "Gloves"

Right Hand Pointing: "Correspondence"

Slipstream: "Burial Clothes"

Switchgrass Review: "Learning Objects"

Tiger's Eye Journal: "Last Rites" & "On Monet's The Red Kerchief Portrait of Mrs. Monet"

West Texas Literary Review: "Old Man in a Rocker"

Zocalo Public Square: "Element"

Early versions of "Gloves" "Letter (crucifixes)" "Letter (key dream)" "The Wall" & "Letter (the wall revisited)" were part of the chapbook, *The Wall* (2012, Tiger's Eye Press).

"Gloves" was also reprinted as part of Ted Kooser's American Life in Poetry column.

Special thanks to my dear friends Adeeba Shahid Talukder and Brian Clifton for close and insightful reads on this manuscript. A warm thanks also to Jeanetta Calhoun Mish for working closely with me in the final edits of the manuscript.

José Angel Araguz is a CantoMundo fellow and the author of seven chapbooks as well as the collections *Everything We Think We Hear* (Floricanto Press) and *Small Fires* (FutureCycle Press). His poems, prose, and reviews have appeared in *Crab Creek Review, Prairie Schooner, The Windward Review,* and *The Bind*. He runs the poetry blog The Friday Influence and teaches English and creative writing at Linfield College in McMinnville, Oregon.

CPSIA information can be obtained
at www.ICGtesting.com
Printed in the USA
LVOW03s1821080318
569141LV00004B/887/P